The Tree of Life

also by Sarah Klassen

Monstrance
The Peony Season
The Wittenbergs

The Tree of Life

poems by

Sarah Klassen

TURNSTONE PRESS

The Tree of Life

Turnstone Press
Artspace Building
206-100 Arthur Street
Winnipeg, MB
R3B 1H3 Canada
www.TurnstonePress.com

Turnstone Press gratefully acknowledges the assistance of the Canada Council for the Arts, the Manitoba Arts Council, the Government of Canada through the Canada Book Fund, and the Province of Manitoba through the Book Publishing Tax Credit and the Book Publisher Marketing Assistance Program.

Cover Art: Terrilynn Goertz

Printed and bound in Canada.

Library and Archives Canada Cataloguing in Publication
Title: The tree of life / by Sarah Klassen.
Names: Klassen, Sarah, 1932- author.
Description: Poems.
Identifiers: Canadiana (print) 20200278827 | Canadiana (ebook) 20200278851 | ISBN 9780888017178 (softcover) | ISBN 9780888017185 (EPUB) | ISBN 9780888017192 (Kindle) | ISBN 9780888017208 (PDF)
Classification: LCC PS8571.L386 T74 2020 | DDC C811/.54—dc23

MIX
Paper from responsible sources
FSC www.fsc.org FSC® C103567

MANITOBA ARTS COUNCIL
CONSEIL DES ARTS DU MANITOBA

Canada Council for the Arts Conseil des arts du Canada

Funded by the Government of Canada
Financé par le gouvernement du Canada
Canada

Manitoba

My worthy friend, gray are all theories,
And green alone Life's golden tree.

—Johann Wolfgang von Goethe

On each side of the river is the tree of life, which produces twelve crops of fruit, bearing its fruit each month. The tree's leaves are for the healing of the nations.

—Revelation 22:2

Contents

VII. Ordinary Time

The Tree of Life

1. Rise and Go

Roads were made for journeys, not destinations.

—Confucius

Bird

A morning mild as milk. Open the window and a bird flies in.
A bird in the house means a death in the house. But this
bird is a finch and your heart is set on pilgrimage.
Gnarled walking stick, a pebble for luck, an open road,
a destination to reach before the sun goes down.

Odd birds those pilgrims hiking to holy Canterbury,
each with a narrative. The gutsy Wife of Bath,
duplicitous Pardoner, eager Squire, Friar with pious passion.
You, too, when you come home—feet calloused,
face burnt by the sun—will spin stories

about the ash heap where the school burned down,
rotting road kill, rising rivers, debris shrouding toppled towers.
Flies intone a dirge around the bruised eyes of children. You'll say
you might have been afraid of death, as every traveller is,
had not that thing with feathers travelled with you.

When the finch begins to sing,
lean hard into the wind
and go.

The Tick of Time

Are we almost there? the children ask.
They are counting SUVs. Red-winged blackbirds
perch like sentinels on posts. The car is a cage,
crops short and green.

Was seeding late this year?
Will pounding rain flatten the grain?
Weeds choke the wheat? Will there be blight?
A plague of locusts? Early frost?

We've fled the city's humid torpor, dull tick of time,
passed almost non-existent towns, single-pump gas stations,
a white wooden church, squat steeple
and a cohort of graves.

Beside a lake, we unpack our loaves and fishes,
unfold the folding chairs.
Already the children's laughter wafts toward us:
music from the water's edge.

The sand is warm and we sleep.
Yellow canola, blue flax blossoms fade,
grain turns from green to gold:
it's harvest time, a dream

from which the screaming seagulls wake us.
We watch the white-capped waves, alarmed
to see our children swimming way beyond their depth.
Come back! we cry,

the offshore wind, the sullen undertow
will pull you deep, drag you from our sight.
We want you here beside us on warm sand.
Come, eat and drink and play with us.

It's getting late. Let's leave
before the sun is low.
Before the headstones cast long shadows
on the grass.

The Road

We laced our hiking boots, grabbed poles,
stowed maps and bottled water in our backpacks.
A flag at half-mast made us pause, not halt.
A siren screamed. Our children asked:
Where are we going? Can we bring the dog?
We slammed the door, shielded our eyes
against the ascending sun.

At any point in time, in one hemisphere or the other, a significant percentage of our planet's more than seven billion people are on the move, travelling on air, land, water, in an overcrowded Zodiac, firm or flimsy aircraft, flat on the wind-buffeted top of a container. They walk on washed-out roads, on burning sand, on bleeding feet, cross tangled jungles, climb mountain trails, bearing the unbearable weight of a piece of bread, coins for something to buy, someone to buy off. Children too sick or too little must be carried on top of the weight of fear: that the overburdened boat will capsize in the ocean swell, pirates will climb on board, the plane will stray into forbidden airspace and mysteriously disintegrate, the train will be derailed, strength will fail. At the border, there will be a wall.

We climbed the narrow trail. Streams of clear water trickled down
from pools we could not see. We sang travelling songs, told stories
about youth and love and bravery. Higher up, the air was thin.
Circling silently, the raptors waited for our steps to falter.
Clouds covered the sun.
Our children were hungry.

We came down from the mountain, entered a forest.
Sunlight filtered through shimmering aspen leaves,
the forest floor gold-dappled. We crossed a river
and arrived at the desert, the land of thirst. Our eyes burned.
Dust filled our mouths. Under our feet, sand shifted.
In this Lenten landscape our children cried for water.
We looked around for palm trees and acacia.
Where are the cypress trees? we wondered.
Where is the tree of life?

Travel Advisory

1.
It happens that a traveller
clutches his thick cloak tight
against the gale-force of the north wind.
Only the noonday sun's warm rays
are able to persuade those rigid fingers
to unclench. Without a hint of protest,
the cumbersome cloak drops to the ground
like a giant beetle's cast-off shell.

2.
Our German teacher reads to us
an ancient ballad:
Die Sonne bringt es an den Tag,
in which the sun, pouring warmth
and light onto the breakfast table,
brings to the man's mind a crime
concealed in his heart; a secret that has torn
and tormented him as he travelled,
brought at last to light. Our teacher says
we should never forget this tale
of guilt and punishment, never
underestimate the sun's power.

A sharp bell rings, books slam shut,
our tongues turn instantly to English.
We race out the door and there
is nothing between us
and the sun.

3.
The sun is a star. Or, if you wish,
a wheel of fire.
In less than ten minutes,
its hot rays reach the place
where children play games
or huddle to plot mischief.
The mother warns her children:
Wear a hat or else
you will burn.

Name

The children want a bigger fire,
sausages for roasting, marshmallows to burn black,
charred sticks, each tip a glowing ember
able to inscribe the midnight sky with messages
as private and as precious as a name.

One morning, on a lakeshore in the Middle East,
an unexpected bonfire. Fish for breakfast.
Nets, worn and waterlogged, spread out to dry.
Around flames and fish, conversation falters.
Nothing dissolves the gloom

that shrouded last night's lake: black sky,
the slow, slow hours. The monotonous
rocking of the fishing boat on troubled water.
Death, burial, the unaccountable
quantity of fish. The questions:

Where do we go from here?
What have we left to hope for?
Who built that fire?

The one who last night, numb with grief
and guilt, announced, *I'm going fishing,*
hears, as the fire dies and lake waves slap the shore,
his name spoken, and the question:
Do you love me?

Our kids have had their fill of sausages;
their hands are sticky and they are tired.
Let's go home, they say.

Rise and Go

1.
A migrant, told by a Voice to rise and go
into untravelled territory, walks with his wife.
His servants and his animals surround him.
He has no son to wrap his arm around.
Night falls. If anyone should ask,
Who are you?
what could he possibly say?
He is far from home, has miles to go,
and does not know the destination.
He pitches his tent and waits for the dawn.

2.
A prisoner in a barren cell asks:
Who am I?
The answer, because death is near, is urgent.
Can years of practising peace, opposing evil, praising love,
ever be proof enough? He's been a good son,
a faithful lover, loves his country. Fellow prisoners
admire his stalwart step, his incredible composure.

But at night, his heart beats at the bars of his confinement;
he is nothing but a broken reed. His knees are weak,
he is sick unto death. He hears the hammer blows
of new construction. A chapel? A house? A gallows.
Before morning breaks he will rise and go,
naked and empty-handed,
to somewhere he has never travelled.

Higher

You yourself are even another little world
And have within you the sun and the moon
And also the stars.

—Origen

Hunger for something more than bread
drives you to rise up, rise higher
to where the air is thin as a newborn's cry,
the view unobstructed. At this height,
solitude will be your soul companion.
You ascend a mountain towering up from wilderness,
climb a ladder, shimmy up a pillar in the desert.
You are prepared to leave behind what you cannot carry
on your back or in your head. You cannot bring the children.
Keep both hands free: one to hold tight,
while reaching with the other for the next rung. Night falls;

silence surrounds you like a wall. Listen to your own breathing,
give ear to the alarm within: a congregation, a quarrelling crowd
of shoppers, a kindergarten class. Wisdom vies with triviality,
doubt with trust. Rage wants to outshout praise.
Are you surprised that you hauled up with you to this altitude
a multitude? The whole world sits at the centre of your self,
waiting to be loved, forgiven, reconciled.
Morning comes. Sun rises.
The desert wind blows sand into your eyes.

In Memoriam

They are no longer with us, cannot walk beside us on the road
or take us by the hand and lead. Emily, whose imagination
valued every slant of light, named hope a thing with feathers.
Etty, who in Westerbork saw beauty everywhere, reclaimed
large areas of peace within herself and reflected them to the world.
Julian of Norwich believed all things would be well.
Chekhov's Sonya told old Uncle Vanya:
We shall rest! We shall see angels!

Ghandi questioned worship without sacrifice,
politics without principle.
Menno argued faith cannot lie dormant; it must feed the hungry,
clothe the naked, shelter the destitute, serve those who harm it.
Martin Luther King Jr. knew darkness cannot dispel light
and only love can drive out hate.
Nelson Mandela knew nothing is impossible with hope.
Some marched in heat toward the salty sea,
some crossed a bridge in boots,
hid in a horse-drawn wagon, were cursed and hunted.
At the lakeshore, a rabbi who prefers to travel light says:
Come, follow me.

Night

Was it what we carried in our heads, a groove worn over time
deep in the brain? Was it tainted blood our hearts pumped
night and day until the whole body pulsed with wanting
everything on offer? Was it the heart itself, overwrought
and desperate? Did darkness make its home there?

They say it is darkest before the dawn,
or in the deepest ocean trough. From the bottom of the well—
into which you have fallen, were thrown, or freely leapt—

raise your eyes to that hemmed-in patch of sky, sunlit by day;
by night, a pitch-black canopy seeded with tiny stars,
crossed by a dying meteor, a wispy comet's tail,
a satellite in endless transit. Look!
The blinking lights of an aircraft coming home to land.

Grounded

The last flight has taken off into the lowering clouds;
the last ferry, half full, is halfway across the water;
no cabs at the taxi stand; both bike tires flat as empty pockets.
And here we are, clutching our maps, our passports,
our children. There must be someone to blame
for failure. There must be a way to hold things together.
We turn, each one, to our devices, send our frustration out
into the world where the climate alters, tectonic plates
grind and shift. As far as we know, the hungry
are still with us. Wars escalate. Bills must be paid.
From time to time, a voice cuts through the pandemonium:
Keep holding, we are told. *Your plight is our priority.*
Someone will be with you soon.
We pace, we smoke, drink coffee.
Our children, after racing, wrestling, quarrelling,
are still not sleepy. They sit in a circle on the ground.
They are playing a game. The girl in the centre is it.

And Yet

The city of refuge is burning.
Smoke and panic fill the air.
Someone says: *Let not your hearts be troubled.*

Words easily spoken. A mantra
to quiet the quaking heart.
A line of poetry.

Fear makes things fall apart.
Knees like water; the heart troubled.
Even a prophet questions the chances.

And yet—beside the brook, the ravens.
And yet—the widow
and the widow's son.

> *Don't be afraid,* the prophet dares to say.
> *Dip into the flour. Tip the jug of oil.*
> *Bake bread as usual.*

Arrivals

On a morning mild and monochrome, we come to the park
to ski. The trail is groomed, wax properly applied;
we get a good glide. Barren birches form a ghostly honour guard.
A patch of black, tattered plastic caught in a forked branch
is a raven scrutinizing us.

We had not planned to think of death, its cold finality.
It is the enemy we want to wrestle down, avoid,
or, if we could, destroy.

Our passage through this wooded park is swift.
We know each twist and turn, know when to swerve
to avoid the oak that always takes us by surprise.
We have never, so far, failed to return whole
to the parking lot. To our SUVs. Our city.
Our very lives.

**

Emerging from the birches, we come to a clearing.
Our trail dips into a snowy bowl just when
the sun burns through the mist and monochrome
gives way to glitter. We are blinded. We blink.
Arranged along the opposite slope of the bowl,
more vision than mirage, a silent, sentient trinity.

We stop in our tracks, trapped by beauty:
three exquisitely sculpted bodies, six alert ears, three
pairs of brown eyes watching us. Who planned this
perfect composition, drew the outline
with a steady hand, gave shape and form,
applied warm colours, breathed life into it?
Who set the schedule for arrival at this moment,
at this indentation? We dare not make a move.

**

In March, a wedge of geese crosses the Lenten sky and veers
to follow the swollen river, edged with ice. They have left home,
are heading north to where the nesting places are. An ancient map
etched in the blood and bones of these returning birds. How else
would they find their way? Their haunting calls announce
the end of another journey. The flock has finally arrived
home.

Refuge

What song do we sing when the journey ends
and we find ourselves in a foreign country
with our exhausted children, our pitiful possessions,
a wardrobe all wrong for the climate,
a language no one understands? Our names
are known to no one, our gestures inappropriate

in this culture. We are naked. Nervous.
The overwhelming welcome breaks our hearts.
Each smile a shocking surprise.
A minivan opens its obedient doors and we ride
like royalty to light-filled rooms, furnished for us.
We are told: *This is your home.*

If we knew the language
and had breath to speak it,
we would ask: *Where is that river*
at whose banks we may fall to our knees
and weep?

New Music

She stands quietly, utterly alert.
When the time is right, she raises her right hand
gracefully, moves her fingers just a little
until sound swells, then lifts her left hand
and this mysteriously controls the pitch.

Music composed of beauty, grace, pure aching
fills earth and heaven with a haunting,
almost-human melody that carries you
on waves of sound, further, higher
than you had hoped to travel

in what years are left to you. You had resigned yourself
to bearing up beneath that same old same old to the end.
But then—this instrument! These skilled hands playing it
with love. Your heart breaks open.
You believe

wonders more amazing than a theremin
(the music streaming from it,
the artist playing it)
will hold the world in place.

> Let every ear be open.
> Let all the earth keep silence.

II. Travelling with Children

... God's kingdom belongs to people like these children.

—Mark 10:14

Travelling with Children
Or: Sermon Series in a Mennonite Church

1.
During our weeks with Moses, we made bricks with straw,
bore the burden of tough quotas,
shrank from each lacerating whiplash.
At night, we listened to the keening of women
who had given birth. We dreamt a saviour
would come and tear us free.

Then we escaped,
thanks to Moses, Aaron, and of course, God.
Miriam composed the praise we loved to sing
sun up, sun down. After the pastoral prayer,
the weekly offering, we compared notes:
which of the plagues had been most cruel,
which most apt, which pharaoh
had we most feared, most hated, wanted dead?

One question troubled us:
Who is this God not one of us has ever actually seen?
Whose hand snatched us from slavery?
Whose voice called us from the river, led us
with flame and fog through wilderness, and left us
bewildered?

2.

Light poured that morning through stained glass.
Rainbow colours fell on us like jewels.
We were told to claim clothes from the closets
of terrified neighbours who said:
Take! Take your unleavened bread and go—
just go!

In the parking lot we debated: lunch at Perkins or Olive Garden?
We marvelled at Divinity's mysterious ways.
How rich we had become.
Never mind our children's restlessness,
the sun's relentless hammering, dry distances
we'd have to plod between departure and arrival,
bearing the weight of plunder.

How quickly in that wilderness
we all grew weary of manna.

3.
Once you've lived beside a river,
you'll always want to rest your burning eyes
on water. Your sore feet crave
immersion in cool currents.

Thirst became our nourishment. Our children,
bored sitting too long under another gush of words,
begged to be released. Sometimes we said yes.
Sometimes we followed them down the aisle
to find a fountain.

It wasn't long before we longed for that river.
We wanted to unsay complaints spoken on its banks.
Confessions stuck to our parched throats, our tongues
too thick with thirst.

We looked for a stream not yet gone dry,
a pool, a puddle. We stopped insisting it must be un-
contaminated, deep enough for immersion.
No one expected to walk on water. Only that it should moisten
the burning lips of our children.

4.
Sunday after Sunday we were at the mercy
of a company of preachers, ordained or lay,
male or female, old, young, educated,
or not so much. All of them
instructing us to set up or collapse
our weathered tents. In that blazing desert
we packed and repacked our possessions,
rounded up our grumbling children.

We wanted an end to wandering. An end to head counts.
We wanted the landscape altered, the sky crammed
with clouds able to deliver rain. We wanted
water running clear through unfrozen pipes,
rust-free, colourless, abundant.

The morning Moses split the rock
we were shocked,
as if in the midst of a church picnic
the heavens opened. That fierce gush
caught us off guard. We expected a hymn.
Announcements. The benediction.

Our children opened their parched mouths
and drank.

5.
One morning, the burning bush became the children's story,
their chance to face the sacred. Our chance to watch their faces
glow as the fire blazed, consuming nothing.
Take off your shoes, we said, and they did.

Trapped in that desert we learned that fire,
when it is hot enough, will melt gold.
Out of gold we reconfigured God.

When Moses climbed down (finally) from the mountain,
his face blazed. We raised our hands
to shield the faces of our children,
then covered our own.

III. Perchance to Dream

Are you sure
That we are awake? It seems to me
That yet we sleep, we dream.

—William Shakespeare,
A Midsummer Night's Dream

Itinerary

This is a foreign country and all roads wind
in ways impossible to follow.
The city in which you find yourself is a dull sprawl,
overpopulated, draped in smog, the buildings
complicated. Endlessly circling and circling,
you find no entrance. Travelling companions blur
and vanish like a summer heat mirage.
The four-star hotel proves impossible
to locate. Even the name of it escapes you.
In a dingy taxi, the dishevelled driver cannot manage
one word of your language. He is unfriendly,
unwilling. You begin to think perhaps you should
begin to worry: Where have you left your cash?
Why have you left your country?
Is your passport in your pocket?
Is it stolen? Left in lost luggage?
Try to think clearly. Where have you packed your shoes?
Why does your favourite jacket no longer fit?
You are holding up the whole, vanished travel group.
Once again you have miscalculated time,
misread departure schedules. Once again
day is waning. Darkness will cover the earth.

Blue

There is a place for everyone
at the table, be it beside father, mother,
those quarrelling sisters, that brother
who died young. A place saved at one end
or the other, along this side or that.

Sadly, you have been replaced
by a growth of elegant delphiniums blooming blue.
Not the blue of sky or lake or flax blossoms.
Not the blue of forget-me-nots
or even your mother's eyes.

There is no name for the subtle shade
that, without warning, has taken your place
at the table. No words were spoken
to comfort you. No one said:
You will be missed.

Window

Something in the classroom has shifted
while your back was turned. Those tall, clever
boys in dark jackets have invented
a brand new game. They do not need you
to explain its aim, rules, etiquette.
While you were listing on the chalkboard
texts to be read, projects due, attitudes
to overhaul, language to shape up
or ban from future use,
the girls left their desks. They are waiting
in line at the window, their summery dresses
radiant in sunlight, their silken haloes
teased by a southerly breeze. While you
add to a list the names of those guilty
of insubordination, tardiness, opinions,
the last pretty girl slips through the open window.
You are just in time to catch a glimpse of one
white ankle sock.

Tower

A man stands on the top of a rickety tower,
high above his brother on a bicycle, his sister
craning her neck. A curious neighbour exclaims
at his iron nerve. Suddenly, vertigo overtakes
the man. He wavers, loses balance. Alarmed,
the neighbour holds a helping hand out to save
the falling fellow who lands hard: skull shattered,
grey matter spilt. The angry brother blames
the neighbour who dared open his mouth to marvel.
Sister is dumbfounded, the tower shaken.

Who was this man? What possessed him to climb so high?
Whose sleep was invaded by this dream
and who will interpret? A mechanical engineer
might ask was that structure made of wood or steel?
An accountant would insist on adding up the cost.
A psychiatrist, if consulted, would shake her head.

Given a handful of crayons, a child draws
the tall tower, a red or yellow bicycle, a daisy
growing bravely up from hard ground, a bunch
of stick figures, their limbs rigid, faces blank.
Can't tell which one is the man whose invisible
nerves of steel snapped before he fell.
Was it the guy who pumps gas on the corner?
The bank manager who authorizes loans? A butcher?
Barber? Stock market analyst? Your own father?

Next, the child draws a river
and beside it a green tree.
In the sky, a cotton cloud
and a small white bird
perched on the tower.

Sting

In a dream, you authorize
the execution by crucifixion
of a man you believe deserving
of such a death. You watch the poor man
writhe on the cross,
struggling and succeeding,
finally,
to tear himself free.

Awake, you rise and go,
distraught, to the window.
It is winter and the tree beside the riverbank,
a rack of bones, mercifully bare
except for an abandoned wasp's nest
that has survived the bitter season.

You were stung once
by a wasp
and did not succumb
to the deadly injection.

Some things you cannot get
your head around. How,
for instance, did that man
escape the cross?

By what means can death
lose its sting?

Where do you get
and how do you execute
authority?

Bus

When once again you board the bus, first class,
built for comfort and speed, tinted windows, take a look
at your fellow travellers, asleep or dreaming, hard to tell
which head holds plans to overthrow the government,
terrorize the world, hijack this bus when it leaves the city
heading into open prairie, hard to tell which bulging bag
in the overhead bin is crammed with contraband, drugs, guns,
honed knives illicitly obtained, forged documents, explosives
ready to detonate, you must not panic, why not close your eyes,
choose your options, count sheep, count countries never visited,
your very favourite things, your many blessings, the bus driver
will turn all the lights off, you must not fear the moonless night,
rumours of war in foreign countries, the huge, hard hands
of the stranger breathing noisily beside you.

Tree

I dreamt a tree, neither pine nor palm,
in a country I had never travelled.
Storms that decimated poplar, birch, and willow
could not disturb its sturdy canopy.
Its fruit ripened where the hungry gathered,
where refugees and strangers rested. I dreamt
a slither in the grass beside a river
that flows through a garden. When I awoke,
the tree woke with me. Its leaves
shone green in vacant spaces of the day,
at the crossroads of simplicity and fear,
lethargy and reconciliation,
alpha and omega.

IV. Angels of Ancient Cities

Where there is ruin, there is hope for a treasure.

—Rumi

Ephesus

1.
Here's where a thing gets turned on its head in the mind
of a man self-named a sinner. He deciphers titles
inscribed on gates to the Agora: *Son of Caesar. High Priest.*
Lord. Titles claimed by VIPs of empire. Divinity a thing
to be grasped. Gloated over. Devotion wrought
by drawn swords, the glint of steel helmets, great snorting horses.

The apostle, unconvinced, squints at the flattery
carved on gates designed and built by slaves once chained
to masters they served with loyalty, intelligence,
engineering skills. Qualities they possessed in measure
greater than those who owned them. The slaves, set free,
paid debts of gratitude they did not owe. In Paul's mind,

honour belongs to a man he never sat at table with
yet knows by heart. A victim of empire, arrested, taunted,
executed. Who, with his last breath, said to a sinner:
Today you will be with me in paradise.
Friends around the table call him master, priest, prince.
They believe his kingdom has begun
to turn the whole damned empire upside down.

2.

Wisdom, in the book of Proverbs, stands unashamed
at the entrance to the city, raises her voice in the street:
instructions to the simple, precepts for pilgrims, the hungry
ushered to a table set with meat and drink. In Ephesus,

Sophia stands restored between two pillars,
shoulders wrapped in a stone shawl, stone eyes fixed
on the unstoppable tsunami: tourists and time
stream past the excavated, reconstructed Celsus Library,

empty of books. A ghost-filled haven.
Croesus had gold enough to fund construction of a temple
honouring Artemis. Demetrius the silversmith
made money making shrines for her.

The wise know speech is silver, silence gold,
and those with ears can hear wind blowing
in the streets of Ephesus. Cypress trees are shaken.
Leaves on the tree of life glow green.

3.
Now as then, we are dismayed when business falters,
baffled when rains fail,
alarmed when another riot erupts in our city.

Now as then, we have among us the hungry. Also
those who regularly bow and bend
and those who don't.

We know a house must have a sure foundation,
a solid cornerstone. We know, though we keep building them,
dividing walls must fall. How else

can the stranger and the alien enter? We do not know
why the angel of peace hovers over there,
while here at home vultures flap hostile wings.

Now as then, noise streams from the marketplace,
applause from the crowded theatre. Listen!
Above the drone of time, the hungry lions roar.

Smyrna

What's in a name?
    The *S* is the sinister hiss of a snake.
    The *m* melts like manna on your lips.
    The *y* merges with an *r* that ripples like a bird-trill.
    The *n* serves to launch, from the tip of your tongue,
    an *a* that is open to anything.

There is poverty in Smyrna,
better seaports elsewhere,
an agora destined to become one more
museum the world won't flock to.

Add to poverty, affliction—and there's more
promised: imprisonment,
persecution to the point of death.

When, in the fine print, it says *crown*,
you may think metaphor.
When it says *don't be afraid*,
stiffen your upper lip.

At the mention of angels, you may see
the shadow of wings
drifting across your city.

Pergamum

1.
Step up on this marble pedestal and rest
your chin on the broken breastplate of this
headless hero overlooking the city—shattered
temples, baths, a precariously steep theatre.

Stretch both arms out: only your hands and wrists
will be visible beyond the armoured chest.
Your head, if you could see it, is no match
for the one gone missing.

The tourist who takes the picture cannot speak
a single word of English, but knows
just what you want. Someone somewhere
will open the photo, smile, and say:

> *Your name, my friend,*
> *may it be carved*
> *on a white stone.*

If ever, while you travel,
you are overcome with hunger, anger,
doubt, a lost passport, listen for the quiet
wind-borne voice that names you, nudges you

past centuries of crumbling pillars, past hope
to where, among the shards, a hoopoe sings.
Here, stoop, dig and pray you'll find
at last the hidden manna.

2.

In this asclepeion, ancient arts of healing
were practised centuries before you were born,
grew up, grew old and ill. Long before
Advil, Prozac, Deltasone.

Patients with fever, broken bones, ailments of spleen,
heart, and mind, roamed freely,
gaped at Trajan's temple, attended the theatre,
strode unrestrained past marble arches

and left. Healed.
It's what we all want:
a return home, body and mind
mended.

Treatment was never onerous. Birdsong
interlaced with music of a cheerful stream.
Long draughts of holy water slowly sipped.
A sweet and spicy pill. A dose of opium.

Come, stroll with me through this dark tunnel.
Don't hesitate. Don't hurry. Don't be afraid.
Light falls on you through clefts
in the stone ceiling. A voice from above,

soft as a feather, elusive as the hoopoe bird,
utters cryptic words of hope,
syllables of comfort you must labour to decipher.
They'll ring incessantly inside your skull,

a tantalizing promise
that will not dissipate,
nor dim,
nor die.

Thyatira

Beauty has enriched the city. Who wouldn't be delighted
to live here, savour rich colours, test with a fingertip
textures of wool, leather, linen. Measure enough
purple fabric for a shawl or shirt. Buy a bronze kettle.

Commerce thrives in Thyatira. Buyers and sellers,
masters and slaves. There are those who grow rich and those
who never escape punishment. Every morning the sun rises,
a fire hot as the eye of God, reflecting off the golden lampstand,

blinding the potter at the kiln. But when darkness falls,
the faithful leave their labour, knowing
they've been promised the morning star.
Knowing an angel guards the tree of life.

Sardis

Not much is left of this fourth-century
stone church barnacled to the broken temple
honouring the goddess Artemis, nor of this
old synagogue, partially restored.

Moonlight dissolves the acropolis. The apostle drifts—a shadow, a ghost—past Roman baths, fragmented capitals of pillars, pagan altars. Past a gymnasium. His sandals are tattered, old cloak stained. He is scouting for a synagogue. He is a man driven. Not by legions of soldiers, unleashed dogs, the searing arc of a steel-enhanced leather lash. A thorn in the flesh invokes the voice that spoke from the light that blinded him. A vision was uncovered in his heart. A summons clear as if it happened yesterday.

You woke this morning to sun and birdsong, but by noon
sky glowers, olive trees crowding the bus window
waver between shimmer and shade. Birds are silent.
The moon's ghost shadows you.

The trumpet voice fell silent in Sardis.
Lampstand empty,
the ancient scroll rolled up,
the angel gone.

Philadelphia

You kept your lamp burning,
whatever the price of oil,
the length of darkness.

Like any flame,
it could have flickered and died,
but never did.

Year after year you toiled,
endured with patience,
stood firm as the new Jerusalem

against all odds.
Your door was always open.
Your light (like your name)
is love.

Laodicea

1.
To the north, Hieropolis has thermal pools
and to the east Colossae boasts cold water.
Here: nothing but tepid. A kind of in-between,
a neither here nor there, a casserole

that's neither raw nor fully cooked,
an argument hardly halfway made, a life
that does not risk yet does not play it totally safe,
but crosses a stone-choked field

where, under the midday sun, red poppies bloom.
The water, when it reaches Laodicea,
whether cold or hot at its source, has become
neither. Adult or child bending to drink

will spit it out. The sheep, thirsty,
lap it up. If the shepherd isn't watching,
a lamb may tumble down the steep
and devious tiers of a theatre

where tragedy and comedy played out
to applause. No one noticed:
the birds had long stopped singing.
Wilderness was closing in.

2.
Located near the old Silk Road,
this city is the place to purchase
goods you have always craved—
above all, gold. The local textile industry
produces snow-white garments.
Grey-green olive trees give oil.

Morning to evening, the plaintive
bleat of vendors' voices: *Come,*
come now, you'd better come
and buy.

3.
This massive indentation, overgrown
with grass whose tiny burrs stick to your socks,
was once a stadium. Athletes came,
trained to run the race, fight the fight,

finish well and ride proudly home
on the shoulders of cheering fans.
The prize:
a perishable crown of laurel.

Behind impregnable doors
of a theatre's not-yet-ruined stage,
ravenous beasts bellow for release.
The savage hunger of lean lions

vies with the steel-edged human cry
of terror—Christian, criminal, coward.
Overriding all, a feral howl:
maws gaping, fisted hands raised.

The ravenous crowd roars exultation,
shouts its extreme joy
across the width and breadth
of wounded centuries.

4.
Who's that knocking
knocking
at my door?

V. Half the Sky

Women hold up half the sky.

—Mao Zedong

Eve

She was there in the beginning,
naked and unashamed,
inspecting fruit trees in God's verdant garden.
Leaves on the tree of life shone green.
A hummingbird sucked nectar from a rose.

We all know what's next:
the polished apple in her outstretched hand.
The taste of it.
A furtive rustling in the grass.

Eve weeps for her children: one son murdered,
the other a murderer. She grits her teeth
against temptation to throw in the towel,
falls to her knees, and with wounded hands
wrings from the grieving earth a garden.

The Concubine

because she was abducted from her home
by a man she didn't know

because she was gang-raped
in a town where all she wanted was
a little rest from travel and some food

because her body was abused,
torn limb from limb, left unburied

because the man whose property she was was out
for revenge, not for her so much as for his own pride

because the story contains scenes of extreme violence
plus more than enough brutal sex for a TV series

and because I've had it with that same old, ugly plot

I will cry out and howl;
I will go about barefoot and stripped.
I will cry out like the jackals,
And mourn like the ostriches.

Is there no balm in Gilead?

Jephthah's Daughter

She has no name, no vote,
no future. Only a brief reprieve: permission
to hike in hill country with her friends.
For two months they are free to dance, sing,
tap their tambourines or wail in chorus
to keep at bay the emptiness of stolen years,
the night of howling jackals.

Hagar

Foreigner. Female. Slave.
With such a resume, what chance has she got

even though she can kill a lamb, cook it,
sweep the floor of the master's tent.

Youth and fertility are both
good news and bad. When all is said and done,

we find her hiding in the desert,
the sun a fireball.

She's not the first woman to find herself
pregnant, alone, facing the essential questions:

Where are you from
and where do you think you're going?

Hot, heavy, afraid,
she faces the Hebrew God, desperate

to know what lies at the heart of this deity
she cannot see. The blazing desert sun

beats down and plain truth dawns:
You are the One who sees me.

The child stirs in her belly.

Esther

Little girls love to dress up
for the festival of Purim:
gauzy gown, golden crown.
Who wouldn't want to be queen for a day?

For Esther, days are long, and nights she is at the mercy
of the king's whim. She could live, or
she could die if she lifts onto her soft shoulders
the burden of a nation's fate.

She gets my vote. Not for the oil, the myrrh,
the perfumed skin or for her readiness to take out
the enemy of her people
or because she is Queen

but because she knows
there is a time for speech, a time for silence,
and she was born
for such a time as this.

Party

She knows no one at the party and comes in anyway,
carrying a jar. (Aren't women always carrying something?
A child, born or unborn, armfuls of washed or unwashed
laundry, a proud or tattered reputation, opinions,
secrets that could accidentally spill.)

Having crashed the party, she breaks the jar,
spilling the aromatic contents, soaking the feet of a man
at the table. Redolence invades nostrils, seeps into
every corner of the room, the conversation. The weeping
woman kneels, towels the fragrant feet with her hair.

Guests are aghast. Such impropriety.
Such tastelessness. The nerve. Besides
(a shrewd guest observes), perfume so costly
should be sold, the proceeds earmarked for the hungry
we have always with us.

He's got a point, hasn't he? He means
the curbside panhandlers we've all cursed,
lineups at food banks, light-fingered
shoppers in produce aisles
of any civilized city.

The man with anointed feet is not from the city.
He's from some fishing village and he's navigated
troubled waters, endured, famished and thirsty,
the predatory wasteland, faced fickle crowds,
faced down the devil, fed the hungry. He knows

the beauty of unleashed extravagance.
Its potency and permanence. The woman's
unseemly sacrifice, the scene created at the party
(he says) will never be forgotten. He knows (and fears)
the future: ancient olive trees, a hill of crosses,

darkness thick enough to swallow hope. He knows
blood will be spilt and he will die,
his body buried like a grain of wheat.
In the morning, the sun will shine,
green spears will pierce the fragrant earth.

Beauty

1.

Rats rustling in the dark, odours of death in every corner.
But you, Etty, on your hard bunk, are still among the living.
Beyond the barracks, beyond barbed wire, you imagine
a field of lupine. An easy leap from that to jasmine
blooming beside a window in Amsterdam
where you rode your bicycle beside the canal,
boarded any tram you pleased, strolled evenings
with your lover past the skating club.

If you cannot sleep it is not sheep you count
but next day's duties. Soup for the mother of a newborn.
Rusks for N who cannot eat hot food. Another letter
to be written (filched paper, borrowed pencil)
to an address in Amsterdam, begging for a coat,
a loaf of bread. Words to a world that will forget,
but is not forgotten in Westerbork. In the morning,
lupine blooming yellow on the heath, you will rise,

take the hand of a terrified child, keep vigil
with an old man's fear of death. Barbed wire is real;
hatred futile. You refuse to the end to give up the anguish
of remembering, feeling, thinking: Dostoyevsky,
Rilke, and the dear man (no longer with the living)
who spoke to you of love, read from the gospels
words that keep you as you keep them in your heart
underneath the yellow star where you store all
the beauty you see everywhere in Westerbork.

2.

The train is waiting. You have packed
your little Bible, diaries, the Russian grammar book,
and Tolstoy. This time
it is *your* name on the list and you must go

east in a baggage car. The overloaded
train will leave; you will arrive
at a destination you refuse to dread,
a place from where no traveller returns.

Will you dare tell those
whose terror and despair crowd the train
that you have looked and always found
life filled with meaning?

Afterwards it will be said:
She left Westerbork
singing.

Cartography

My mother grabbed a piece of cutlery and with it mapped
a world on the oil-cloth-covered table. It might have been
right after supper, sun gliding toward the horizon. Or
the morning of a school day timetabled for history.
She drew a distant, different world, a place that was
invisible to me. The grassy bank beside a railroad track,
the train's whistle keen as silver. A river. The summer
sweetness of watermelon concealed beneath
a tough green rind.

                              Was that river deep?
The train late leaving? She would point her fork and say:
Here stood three houses in a row, ours the middle one.
I did not ask if rain was falling on the houses,
on grass beside the railroad track. When the train left,
were young men leaning out the windows, waving
to young girls singing on the grassy bank? Perhaps
a breeze cooled the air, cooled the blood.

                              My mother holds her fork steady,
listens for one more shriek from a train already out of sight.
The pretty girls sink to their knees on damp grass.
The railroad track sinks into memory. Gunfire dies,
the young men home again. Or gone. My mother gone.
Long gone that map she sketched: a construct of desire,
each detail filtered through memory's imperfections,
the vagaries of space and time.

                              That house, she said,
was made of brick. And solid. We left it on a morning
filled with sorrow.

Reading Sylvia Plath

One summer I read Sylvia Plath, her late and early poems,
letters home, biographies and what the critics wrote
about her talent, marriage, forays into beekeeping,
utter darkness. A mourning dove claimed a perch
in a branch of the ash tree under which I lounged,
tackling one more point of view, another analysis.
I was forming my own opinion of Plath, who crawled
under the steps, waded far out into dark water.

The bright sun hurt my eyes. I was distracted by the dazzling
wings of a dragonfly, cloying scent of petunias, shrill bell
on the bike of the ice cream boy. It was a hot summer
unrelieved by rain. I read past yew trees. Tulips. I arrived
at the sealed-off room, food left for the children, gas turned on.
(The mourning dove had built her nest elsewhere.)

A Death in the City

The woman in the coffin loved to be tucked in
at bedtime, sun long gone, the drab city
lit up like an amusement park, the bold glare
of headlights slicing the gloom of our saddest
avenues. The gnarled and knotted
hands that, with a mother's tenderness,
drew the sheets up over her arms and shoulders,
tucked them under her chin, stroked the tired brow,
belonged to her husband. She was his
helpmate, soulmate, housekeeper. The whole world
had been modernized, electronically enhanced,
economically shaken, stabilized, or terrorized.
Wars waxed and waned, glaciers melted, honeybee
populations dwindled and so many mayors were elected
during threescore years and ten of marriage. There was joy
at a child's first cry, first smile, each small, firm fist.
City crews lit up the tree in front of city hall.
Any day now, snow will fall. They say
the woman's smile was sunshine, she loved cooking,
loved singing *Müde bin ich, geh' zur Ruh*
with her husband. When she closed her eyes,
he stroked her furrowed forehead, sang to her
with a quavering voice, intoned
without a trace of haste or anguish:
God bless you and keep you. And then
he let her go.

Country

This woman has come from another country.
She's left behind moist valleys, the spicy scent
of her mother's cooking. Her sister's smile.
Voices she grew up with echo hauntingly.
She holds my feet in her gloved hands,
bows her gleaming head as if in sorrow.
Her slender fingers grip my toes, ankles, calves.
She scrubs with vigour, kneads and slaps my legs

and offers me a multitude of colours:
burnt orange of sunset (her country or mine),
coral like her lips, pink like the palm of her hand,
black like her hair. I want her to name the precise shade
for happiness. I want her to tell me
she has found it in this country.

VI. Alpha and Omega

There's a season for everything
and a time for every matter
under the heavens ....

—Ecclesiastes 3:1

Alpha and Omega

Let there be light! A flash, a bolt, a brilliant blaze
that puts the kibosh on chaos. Let light shine on width, breadth,
depth, a dazzle to illuminate all matter everywhere. Let it glint
gloriously off ocean wave, sea swell, a brooklet's little ripples.

Let fish rejoice in it fantastically, the fur of fox, cat, cougar,
coyote be haloed. Let light's hot pulse pull prairie grass and
milkweed up to verdant growth, turn grain from green to gold.
In every garden everywhere let peonies, preposterous

begonias unfold. Let every butterfly, bat, bird bathe in radiance.
Let light pour mornings into breakfast bowls, fill empty cups
to overflowing. At evening, let light's mauve plumes linger
on every atom of creation. When darkness closes in,

shrouding the valley floor,
let sky be spangled still, lit with the glow of meteors,
the murky Milky Way, the white-hot stars. O Light of life,
Light of the wobbling world: your splendour does not tarnish,

will not be overcome by random avalanche,
smart missile, guns, flood, smoke of forest fire.
You melt the iron grip of fear. The stone-cold,
guarded grave can never hold you.

The Week

On Monday, you believe beauty will save the world.
By mid-week, the latest interactive art installation,
new music, your most heartfelt poems
have accomplished nothing. On Saturday—drizzle,
followed by hard rain.
                                        Stopped at a red light
on Main Street, potholed after winter,
you fall prey to panhandlers hoisting rain-dampened
cardboard pleas. You avoid eye contact,
gesture toward the soup kitchen at the corner.
                                        Light changes and you turn
toward the greenhouse where the air is redolent
with April. A radiance of red geraniums,
a tantrum of petunias, Celebrity tomatoes
guaranteed to ripen early.
                                        On Sunday,
rain has stopped. Sun rises and you also rise
and raise your voice in gratitude
for earth's bright beauty. For the sky
that poured down water.
                                        High time
to bury the fragile roots of seedlings in wet earth.
You'll need gloves, trowel, boots,
and sturdy padding for your knees.

Advent

I wake to a world riddled with mystery:
darkness shot through with the first ray of light.
December and still,
still the ladybug wants in. Wants to shelter
in that thin place between
glass and the wooden frame of the patio door.

**

Look: a table spread with star-shaped, sprinkled
sugar cookies, a shimmer of delight.
Who knows what this portends, what miracle
it points to? Something
is pending. Any minute now the mystery
will be at last revealed. Perhaps
not wholly understood,
but wholly holy.

**

Suppose God is not dead but buried
in the warm depth of a female body,
waiting
for the auspicious moment
to enter the time between
this and the darkness
of that other burial.

**

The final postal code is written,
the last e-card sent.
Rugs are vacuumed, the tree adorned,
four candles lit.
What else, what else must I do?
When will all be ready?
When, at last, will I?

Magnificat

Snow has fallen overnight on roofs of suburban bungalows,
on stiff spirea hedges, on rows of overflowing garbage bins.
Blackbirds occupy a snow-lined poplar branch. Magnificent
in winter white are five wolves cast in bronze
and set in fierce pursuit beside the freeway.
                                        In Bethlehem
there is no snow. Pilgrims armed with bucket lists
crowd the place where twenty centuries ago
they believe a boy was born. The amazed girl-mother
nestled him in straw: a child as perfect as a snowflake.
                                        Mary never knew
the crunch of snow beneath her feet. Sleet
needling her face.
                                        What she was given to know
poured from her mouth like praise. The destitute,
she dared to say, will not always hunger and thirst,
nor will the meek be scattered.
What's high will be brought low.
                                        She might as well have said
bronze wolves will be set free,
spirea hedges shout loud Hallelujahs,
and snow-capped lids of garbage bins
clap noisily for joy.

Incarnation

God is carnal? Yes. God
has got to be flesh and blood.
Bones, too,
like any one of us. A child
can't go to sleep in a dark room
unless someone is right there
beside her: someone
with some skin.

Boxing Day

A fox, alone, motionless on the frozen river.
It is the Feast of Saint Stephen. Just yesterday,
Christ was born in Bethlehem. At the new Ikea,
doors open and the long line holding vigil moves
from cold to warmth, from darkness into light.

On the day of execution, Saint Stephen's face
wore the radiance of an angel. On this bitter morning,
breath is visible, uncovered skin freezes within minutes.
Monarch and faithful page stride forth through storm.
Does the boy, knee-deep in his master's footprints, know

a gift is not so much to get but to give? The silver
moon grows pale in the light of the rising sun
and children, warm from bed, play fox and geese
in the frozen garden. At last the fox's mate appears
and, like two thoughts in motion, they lope north

together. The children, summoned to supper,
abandon their snow angels. Spent shoppers
haul their boxed burdens home.

Feast of the Holy Innocents

How shall we observe the day
a tyrant, driven by rage,
unholy fear of losing power or face,
unleashed slaughter?

We are too outraged to pray.
Too downcast for singing.
Tears are futile, the usual
wringing of hands pathetic.
Rage cannot bring back the dead
nor save the living. We know

we should unclench our fists,
take each other by the hand,
light candles,
and with one voice
speak reverently
the sacred names

of those who hunger and thirst.
Who flee but can never escape.
Who wait in vain at borders
with their hungry children.
The names of those who have lost
or never had.

Sadly, we don't know their names
and, if we did, might mispronounce them.
We want to hold them—like we hold
these burnt-down candles—with unsteady hands
in our unsteady hearts.

Myrrh

Three times the prince of peace,
almighty God, the everlasting father
is given the gift of myrrh. The first,

at birth, an event commemorated
in winter with papier-mâché camels,
decked-out trees and jingle bells in every mall.

Fast forward to the day the prince is lifted high,
a chalice raised to his dying lips: wine
laced with sedating myrrh.

The saviour—come to bear,
not sidestep, suffering—
refuses it.

On the third occasion, Nicodemus
comes at night, bringing the costly spice
to embalm the body lowered from the tree.

Sealed in the guarded sepulchre
in darkness, Jesus rests.
The rest is mystery

or miracle. The impossible
weight of the stone. The empty cave.
The lingering fragrance of myrrh

and the women's grief
turned to joy.

Egg

The goose that laid the egg lies flat
on the gravelled ledge overhanging the entrance.
A hard bed for birth. The gander stakes out space
in the featureless parking lot from where he eyes
goose and egg. The shining oval is not golden;
it is white and large and holds within its fragile skin
the future. The door opens: a child emerges
and a woman with the slow pace of Parkinson's.
They do not see the goose that laid the egg.
They see the gander stretching his elegant neck,
impatient for the shell to break open
the way the sun (while child and woman slept)
broke through night's darkness to release
the first gold shaft of light.

Ritual

Holy Week and three buffleheads on the cold river
practise the rite of baptism. Their preference:
complete immersion. Again and again they duck
and disappear into ice-cold darkness, then emerge, shaking
a zillion stars from their feathers.
        As if there is never enough,
they plunge down deep and rise and dive
and rise again.
        The week winds down, down, down
toward Friday. Temple draperies are torn.
Darkness enfolds the earth. The dead in their stone tombs
have begun stirring as if, like the sun in the morning,
they, too, will rise.

Calendar

We've entered ordinary time, left behind
incarnation, crucifixion, resurrection, and *ascension,*
words rooted in Latin and set like stones
on which belief rests. We've stowed the straw
manger, shepherds' crooks, the sparkling star,
papier-mâché camels. But not the cross
our kids constructed out of popsicle sticks,
one side painted black, the other crayoned

unrestrainedly. The flames of Pentecost
(a flicker from the Greek) do not die down
in times of extraordinary weather, the rise or fall
of presidents, the unstable price of oil.
In ordinary times, those tongues of fire
whirl like fervent dervishes and dance.

VII. Ordinary Time

Nature does not hurry, yet everything is accomplished.

—Lao Tzu

Click

A twin-tufted owl sat unperturbed on the corner
of a garden fence. I took a picture. End of story?
Or a story in search of an ending?

Not every narrative begins at the beginning. Of course,
we like a good first paragraph, first sentence, first word.
The second time I saw the great horned owl,

I knew that if I touched the silent bird
with my coffee cup or credit card,
plastic would click on plastic.

Between the two sightings, I'd posted the picture
on Facebook. Now there's nowhere it can't go.
Nowhere I can hide.

Owls are said to be wise. Wisdom
cannot be caught on camera, nor does it catch you
by surprise. Had the owl blinked

would that have made a better story?
Would you have clicked "like"?

Fear

Of all wild things, the sparrow
—unkempt body, claws
like little commas, those
ridiculously tiny bones,
that brash bird-chirp—

is most known for industrious foraging,
effortless flitting
morning to nightfall,
bush to bush.

Sparrows are sold
two for a penny in the temple.
We are told how easily
and frequently they fall
though never unseen.

Of all qualities to fear,
the endearing fearlessness
of a dun-feathered,
sassy sparrow
is most terrifying.

Blink

The morning park is colourless:
white bark of birch
black oak
poplars in shifting shades of grey
sullen and mute as the sky.

No chatter of chickadees
no clattering branches
not even rustling leaves
and no disturbance of squirrels.

Don't be fooled.

Stasis is not absence.
Silent deer—ears taut—wait
camouflaged behind bare branches of hawthorn.
A bird with a song in its throat lurks in a hazel bush.

Silent within this motionless monochrome
the sentient world stares back at you.
Who will be first to blink?

Be Alert

Watch Out! Stay alert!
—Mark 13:33

Cat on the lookout for some small morsel:
bird or butterfly. A mouse. Wasps
nuzzle the patio's torn screen door, seeking refuge
from autumn wind, the swirling poplar leaves.

What is it I should watch for and where?
My neighbour, mistrusting social media,
watches for the mailman. The news he brings,
she believes, may sometimes be, but is not always, fake.

Our children wait for the ice cream boy
as earnestly as legal experts waited
for Jesus to fumble answers to questions
meant to do him in. Millennia later,

scholars remain wary of the apostle:
Did he hate women? What about
that thorn in the flesh he was so cagey about?
What really happened on the road to Damascus?

The river reflects the golden glow of elm leaves,
the red of Amur maple. O may I be alert
to light that blooms in every bush,
illuminates the purring cat.
The torn screen door.

Eagle

1.

A bald eagle in transit across the sky's blue canopy.
The large bird turns and spirals elegantly down, down,

then, rising on currents of air, soars like an organ chord
across the river and lands on the branch of an oak.

If, as the song says, we'll rise one day on wings of an eagle,
will those curved talons remain hidden, that beak clamped shut?

At the concert, a woman in a sky-blue dress moves her hands,
elegant as winnowing birdwings, draws from her instrument

a melody pure as the human voice. Not touch but motion
lures music from a theremin. How gracefully

those skilled hands move. How doggedly
those eagle talons grip the gnarled branch.

2.

On a pan of river ice, a black hulk crouches over its kill.
Blood stains the snow. Tenacious talons won't let go.

The sharp beak tears at the flesh of a fish;
the eagle feasts and leaves the rest to a crow.

Rising on hinged wings, head gleaming like a beacon,
the majestic bird draws circle after circle around carrion and crow.

A white feather, the weight of waning melody,
sails down to the river.

Breakfast with Elephants

A cattle egret in the grass.
A lumbering clan of elephants, grazing.
In the distance, a line of low blue hills.

O what a beautiful morning.

The spacious sky. Forward-propelling wind.
Our pilot able to persuade the roaring flames
to lift us up and set us down

on solid ground. Someone has laid out silverware,
glassware, a clean white cloth.
Can you believe it? we say to each other,

A table set for all of us in the presence of elephants.

Corks pop. Champagne is poured.
The huge balloon lets out its last big breath.
The low blue hills have melted into the distance.

Fulfilment

These geese have accomplished what they were born for:
tedious flight north, nest-building on a riverbank,
eggs laid and warmed. Not least the long
days of waiting for shells to crack and voilà!
The expected surprise. On murky river water,

goose and gander float regally with the current,
trailed by the fruit of their goose labour, goose love.

A crow couple clamped to a willow branch.
Four jet eyes nail the goslings, a succulent quartet
that sooner or later will amble up the muddy bank.
The crows rehearse a hoarse *caw, caw, caw,*
hone beak and claw, practise surprise dives

to disperse goose and gander. With lethal speed,
the crows accomplish what they were born for.

In Passing

Before sundown on a spring evening,
I leaned over the balcony railing. Below me,
the river slithered north, a grey-green, turgid serpent.
A vulture soared, hungry gulls dropped down
from the sky. As if from an old myth,

six half-grown foxes came, yelping, chasing,
wrestling on the grass like children unrestrained
by fear of predators or vixen mother
or time too swiftly passing. I knew
the joyful interlude would end. Suddenly

as they had come, they left. I wanted them
to stay with me. Next night and the next,
I came like Roxanne to my balcony,
not for the silver moon, not for poetry,
but for a whirl of fur in grass,
hot animal breath.
Those sharp yips of joy.

Hope

In the morning, I come to the window to escape
slaughter in dark Africa, Armageddon in the Middle East,
a rapist at large in my neighbourhood.

The river has not stopped flowing north
to the lake; gulls are scavenging; buffleheads diving.
I have reason to hope

I may catch sight of the coyote loping along the bank.
A hawk hovers, hungry, wings wide open
as if in benediction. It is time for breakfast:

dry cereal, milk from the fridge, an orange bright as the sun.
Radio off, kettle on, I breathe words of gratitude
and pray the wary coyote, rising from sleep or hunger,

will drag his wild shadow out of the willows,
down to the river.

Heading Home

A small flotilla of gulls on the muddy river,
their grey wings altered by alchemy of autumn sun
to silver, their outraged voices hushed.
They are at home on water, at home in the sky.

Upriver, a convoy of geese contemplates, courageously,
the next long flight. Flapping, they lift off and aim
their trademark pattern south. Are they going home?
Or is home north where the nests are?

Home is where the graves are, someone wrote.
I will visit today the grave of a friend who flew
too soon from home and landed
elsewhere. The predatory gulls swoop up,

screaming. Aloft, they circle, circle, plummet,
plunge. Is the airborne honking of wild geese
alarm or is it joy for the journey
of birds? My friend said, wistfully,

as we watched a flock of cedar waxwings
plunder the ash tree in autumn:
They are fuelling up.
They are preparing to fly home.

String

A creature ablaze with colour rides toward you,
golden helmet, emerald coat.
A conquering hero? Emissary from a nobler world?

Perched like a monarch on a man's grey-shirted shoulder,
the exotic bird ignores skateboarders, dads with kids
on tricycles, dog-walkers, city crews planting lilac trees.

Won't it fly away? you ask.
This isn't an it, the man says, bristling. *She's a female*
Yellow-Headed Amazon from Guatemala or Belize.

A standoff in the heat of Ethiopia. Syrian refugees
trapped in camps in Lebanon. Above you, clouds colliding.
There's a string attached to one thin leg of the bird,

one end looped around the man's middle finger.
Where does that phrase, *No strings attached,* originate?
Is the beautiful bird in bondage or secure within fixed limits?

Looks like she's poised for flight. Away from noise of traffic,
away from the human shoulder, the leashed dogs. Look at her
stretch that golden neck, unfold those bright green feathers.

Just watch her scale the perfectly aligned lilac trees,
catch an updraft and ascend like the sun to the sky.
She's going home

to Guatemala or Belize
a free bird,
trailing a long, thin string.

Emergent

A shadow falls on the wall of the tool shed.
Something indefinable is struggling to crawl up,
but the metal wall is too smooth. I lean a two-by-four
against the shed. The awkward thing finds foothold
on the wood, moves cautiously up, up toward the light.
It has no actual feet but the body about to emerge
has beginnings of extensions: like latent limbs. Is this
phenomenon I'm watching an emergency? Is it magic?
Might this be a miracle, impossible to document,
though I bring paper, pen, and camera to record
what I objectively observe? The emergence proceeds,
a slow splitting. The clumsy entity's original configuration
alters: filmy wings take shape and spread, wet and fragile.
The sun's warmth sucks them dry.
If I am patient, I will witness lift-off,
a newborn moth weightless as helium
or a prayer released, unbidden:
O God, let not the local crows or that red squirrel notice.
Let not the neighbour's cat come creeping.

The Visit

At evening, deer come softly to the garden
bringing nothing but their hunger and their grace.
Light as shadows, they leap over the wire fence,
planting their delicate hoofs between young rows
of lettuce. Grace and the fierce hook of hunger
entitle them to the earth's plenitude. They chew
what hands with hope and labour planted,
what sun and rain have wrung from soil and seed.

It's morning and the apple tree has lost a ring of bark.
Lettuce grazed down to the nub. Snap peas gone.
We're left with heart-shaped imprints,
those bald patches, and piles of brown pellets
to nourish the earth. The deer have left us
grounds for hope. Reason to begin again.

Trees

1. Apple

Apples in the Song of Solomon
are metaphors for love, they say. I say
they were plucked from a real tree
a real axe could fell. Imagine

the delight of discovering
an apple tree in Eden,
blossoming and bearing fruit
not far from the tree of life.

Amy Lowell wrote a poem about apples
in the garden of the Hesperides.
She has them glimmering, glowing,
glittering, gold.

Pursued, Atalanta knew she could outrun
the most impassioned suitor. She was swift and wisely
warned by the oracle. But when the first
bright apple dropped, she bent to pick it up.

My neighbour, old, arthritic, nearly blind,
can't climb the ladder propped against the trunk.
She sends me up into the leafy canopy
to pick a basketful of fruit from which

she bakes a perfect pie.
We eat it, seated side by side
on a bench beneath the apple tree.

2. Oak

A branch of our oak had grown thick and bent
into something resembling the handle of an oversized cup
a giant could stick his fat thumb through.
An extra appendage. A deformity we made rude jokes about.

When our city cousins came, that rough, ridged trunk
became a mast the boys climbed up like veterans.
They straddled the wayward branch and from that vantage point
overlooked the world. It was summer. Somewhere far away

war was raging. Another Spitfire blasted from the sky,
another battleship gone down. Dad and the uncles,
pacifists all, huddled in the house, arguing:
Who will lose? Whose side might God be on?

The aunts made peace: they left their babies
sleeping in the bedroom. One small peep
sent someone running. Sweat ran from Mother's face.
I'll bet there's shade beneath the oak, she said.

The boys on the bent branch aimed invisible weapons
at the enemy. Sharp bursts of gunfire flew from their throats.
Girl cousins burst like barely opened blossoms from the house.
The boys declared them dead. Dad left his city brothers

to decide the war. It was time for chores.
Mother and the aunts laid out lunch.
The boys were angry at the girls for being
alive, dancing under the old oak tree

while hawks with outspread wings
carved circles in the sky.

3. Spruce

An antlered deer hangs from a spruce branch
overhanging the ski trail. I wonder who—
after packing skis, poles, scarves, and kids
into the minivan—would think of bringing a Christmas
ornament to hang on a branch skiers must duck under to avoid
getting needled in the eye. Snow blinds me
as I glide along the groomed trail. The small
suspended deer glides with me. Together
we round bends, fishbone up slopes,
swoosh down the other side and arrive
at the parking lot.
                                        One week later,
the December sun limps along roofs and treetops;
the highway is icy. I've got two stars in my pocket.
Two lengths of string. One star above the deer
and one below, or one on either side? The slick trail
speeds me to the wayside spruce, adorned
last week with one small deer, today bedecked
with a multitude of silver bells, glittering icicles,
red velvet bows, three angels, wings outspread.
I pull two crumpled stars from my pocket
and hang them on the tree.

4. Sycamore

Its bark peels back like curled scales
of a large fish. The dome-shaped canopy
gives shelter and shade. The ragged
five-lobed leaves create a camouflage
and twigs make zigzag patterns. Fruit is wooden,
round as marbles children love to trade.
In the abundance of helicopter seeds,
the sycamore's future rests.
                                                    Climb up
into the leafy hiding place: the radiant
sky above, earth spread out below.
Someone on the pavement, craning,
catches the hunger in your eyes.
A voice like wind from the east calls up:
You there! Come down! It's time to eat!

5. Fig

Sunlight streaming through stained glass
falls on the pew like jewels.
The gospel someone reads invites you
to find yourself inside the parable
about a barren fig tree.
(Not one single fig this year!)

Which role is right for you?

Are you the owner of the orchard,
impatient for quick profit,
incensed at unproductive time and toil?
Does your mind incline toward wealth
management? A trip to the bank?
A Caribbean cruise?

No? That's not you?

The gardener, then?
Last year you grew a beet the size of a child's head,
harvested more beans than you could give away,
filled jars with sauce and salsa.
But you say you've never been, nor plan to be
an arborist? Perhaps

you are that hapless fig tree,
offered a last-minute reprieve
by the master of second chances.
Your roots will be rudely disturbed.
Fertilizer comes with an acrid stench.

Don't turn down the role.
Things could be worse.
It could have been a text
about expulsion from the garden
that someone read while the sun shone
and coloured light fell into your lap.

6. Green

That tree with the crimson circle on its bark
is marked for destruction, doomed
by Dutch elm disease. The emerald ash
borer has moved into our neighbourhood.
We are afraid. We scour the internet to find
salvation for our city's canopy: a rot-resisting
species we might import if our winters weren't so long,
our summers not so dry, our resources not spent
on fractured infrastructure, drug deaths,
healthcare chaos, and how many refugees
before we slam the door.
                                                            The tree we want
grows beside streams of water where its roots
go deep and drink. Its leaves are always green.
From its pinnacle, the eagle watches the world.
In its branches, the sparrow builds her nest.

Notes

All Bible quotations throughout are from the Common English Bible, copyright 2011 and are used with permission.

"Rise and Go"—The migrant is the patriarch Abraham and the prisoner is Dietrich Bonhoeffer.

"Travel Advisory"—*Die Sonne bringt es an den Tag* means "The sun will bring it to light."

"The Concubine"—This story is found in Judges 19. The quotations in this poem are from Micah 1:8 and Jeremiah 8:22.

"Beauty"—Westerbork was a transit camp in Holland during WWII. Etty Hillesum volunteered at Westerbork before she was sent to Auschwitz.

"A Death in the City"—*Müde bin ich, geh' zur Ruh* means "I'm tired and going to rest."

The section titled "Angels of Ancient Cities" is based on the seven cities in Revelation 2 & 3. These sites are currently in various stages of ruin and/or excavation and reconstruction.

Acknowledgements

I'm grateful to the team at Turnstone Press for diligence, thoughtfulness, and precision in helping *The Tree of Life* grow from manuscript to book. Thanks to Melissa McIvor for attending to much more than just the mechanics of the text, to Terrilynn Goertz for the cover art, to Jamis Paulson for the cover design, and to Alice Major for her discerning edits.

Poems in this collection have appeared in *EXILE*, *Christian Century*, *CV2*, *Image*, *Prairie Fire*, *McMaster Journal of Theology and Ministry*, *The New Quarterly*, the *Winnipeg Free Press* and in the anthologies, *The Turning Aside* (ed. D.S. Martin) and *Heartwood* (ed. Lesley Strutt).

"Travelling with Children" and "Beauty" received the National Magazine Awards' Silver Medal for Poetry. The sequence in "Perchance to Dream," was shortlisted for the Gwendolyn McEwan Prize. Poems from "Rise and Go" were shortlisted for the Ross and Davis Mitchell Prize.